Splish, Splash, Foxes Dash!

Geraldo Valério

CANADIAN
WILDLIFE
IN COLOUR

Owlkids Books

Red,
yellow,
blue,
here they come...
Canadian animals
in colour!

RED

Cardinals
perch
and peck

BROWN

Under water, **duck** dabbles

ORANGE

Among
pumpkins,
foxes
hide and seek

Mountain goat
warm
in a woolly coat

WHITE

Around flowers, bees buzzzzz

YELLOW

GREEN

Hungry
caterpillars
lunch on
leaves

Big, BIG, BIG blue whales

BLACK

Bears
breakfast
in a
bed of
berries

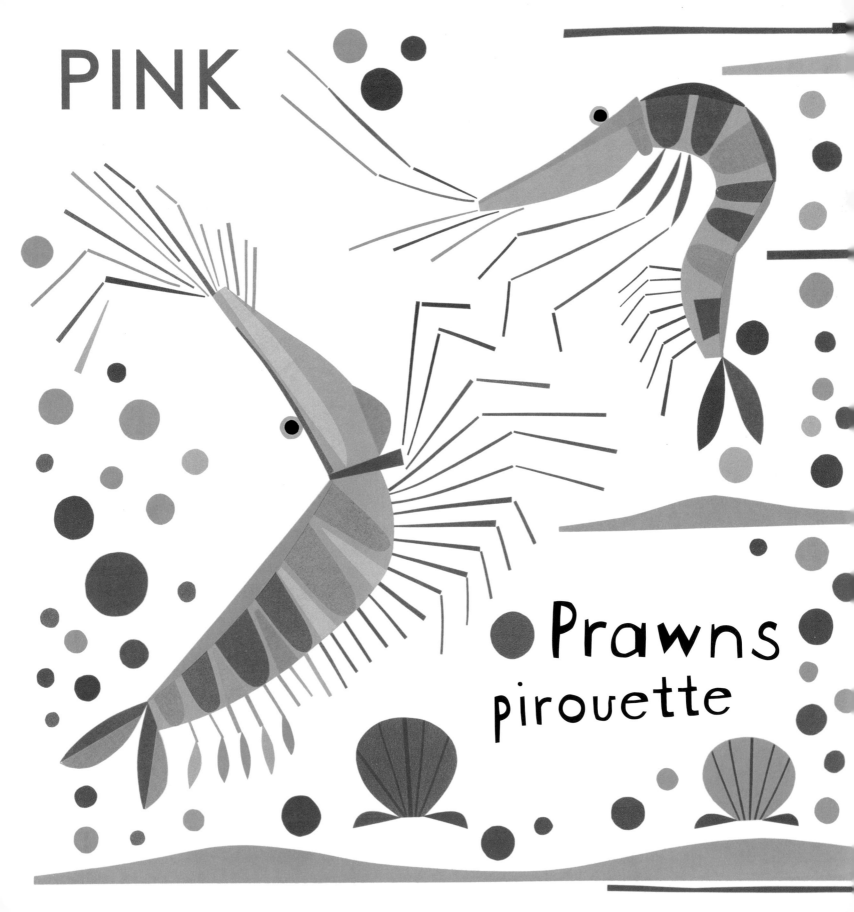

PINK

Prawns
pirouette

PURPLE

Sea
stars
stretch

Seal
pup
safe and
snug

GREY

Red

Northern Cardinal

Cardinals don't fly south for the winter. A feeder stocked with sunflower seeds will attract the bright red male and the pale brown female with their eye masks and pointy head crests.

Brown

Northern Pintail Duck

This duck is a dabbler: It tips tail up, head down, in shallow water, to forage for food. Using its long neck to reach the muddy bottom, the bird feeds on seeds, plants, aquatic insects, crustaceans, and snails.

Orange

Red Fox

Wow-wow-wow! That's the sound this fox makes as it approaches another red fox. These mammals can make as many as twelve different sounds, which they use to greet and "talk" to each other. Red foxes are usually orangy-red, but can also be golden, brown, black, or silver.

White

Mountain Goat

The mountain goat's feet help it climb and leap surely and nimbly on rocks, cliffs, and ice. Rough pads on the bottom are good for gripping; cloven hooves act like two toes that spread apart for balance.

Yellow

Bumblebee

This insect's yellow and black colours warn other animals to keep away, because the females can sting. But there's no need to worry: Bumblebees aren't aggressive and only sting to protect themselves.

Green

Luna Moth Caterpillar

After it hatches from an egg, this caterpillar goes through five stages, during which the larva eats and grows and sheds its skin. When threatened, it can rear up, make a clicking noise with its mandible, and vomit fluids to scare off an attacker.

Blue

Blue Whale

When blue whales breathe, they surface, open their blowholes, and exhale in one powerful breath. But what you see is not a waterspout. The warm air exploding from their lungs mixes with water and creates a column of mist that is taller than a giraffe.

Black

American Black Bear

Black bears eat a lot of berries—as many as 30,000 a day! They scoop them up with their lips and swallow them whole. Experts can tell what kinds of berries these mammals have been eating by examining the seeds in their scat.

Pink

Northern Prawn

Prawns, or shrimp, swim forward by paddling with their swimmerets—the small paddle-shaped pairs of legs on the underside of their abdomens. To escape from danger, these crustaceans flick their tails, which moves them quickly backwards.

Purple

Purple Sea Star

The purple sea star has five arms. Other kinds of sea stars can have more: ten, twenty, or even as many as forty!

Grey

Grey Seal

Seals are marine mammals. They spend most of their time in the water, coming out only to mate, give birth, molt or shed, and get away from predators.

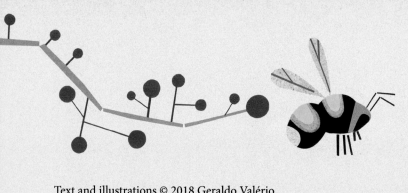

Owlkids Books acknowledges the financial support of the Canada Council for the Arts, the Ontario Arts Council, the Government of Canada through the Canada Book Fund (CBF) and the Government of Ontario through the Ontario Media Development Corporation's Book Initiative for our publishing activities.

Published in Canada by
Owlkids Books Inc.
10 Lower Spadina Avenue
Toronto, ON M5V 2Z2

Published in the United States by
Owlkids Books Inc.
1700 Fourth Street
Berkeley, CA 94710

Library and Archives Canada Cataloguing in Publication

Valério, Geraldo, 1970-, author, illustrator
    Splish, splash, foxes dash! : Canadian wildlife in colour / written and illustrated by Geraldo Valério.

ISBN 978-1-77147-290-6 (hardcover)

    1. Color--Juvenile literature. 2. Animals--Canada--Pictorial works--Juvenile literature.
I. Title. II. Title: Canadian wildlife in colour.

QC495.5.V35 2018   j535.6   C2017-907420-2

Library of Congress Control Number: 2017961190

The artwork in this book was rendered in paper collage.
Edited by Debbie Rogosin
Designed by Claudia Dávila

ONTARIO ARTS COUNCIL
CONSEIL DES ARTS DE L'ONTARIO
an Ontario government agency
un organisme du gouvernement de l'Ontario

Canada Council
for the Arts

Conseil des Arts
du Canada

Canada

Manufactured in Shenzhen, Guangdong, China, in March 2018, by WKT Co. Ltd.
Job #17CB2682

A   B   C   D   E   F

OWL kids

Publisher of Chirp, chickaDEE and OWL
www.owlkidsbooks.com

Owlkids Books is a division of

Bayard
CANADA